ORIGAMI SAFARI

STEVE AND MEGUMI BIDDLE

Illustrated by Megumi Biddle

Tupelo Books   New York

ABOUT THE AUTHORS

Steve Biddle is a professional entertainer with a specialty act that has taken him all over the world. He studied origami in Japan with the top Japanese origami masters, thereby acquiring deeper knowledge of a subject that has always fascinated him. Megumi Biddle is a highly qualified graphic artist, designer, and illustrator with a long-standing interest in paper and its many applications.

Steve and Megumi combine their talents to design items for television, feature films, and major advertising campaigns, and in writing books for children and adults.

They have taken their craft all over the United States to schools, festivals, and arts centers and currently present a weekly origami program for cable television.

First published by Random House UK, Ltd., as a Red Fox Book.

First American edition published 1994 by Tupelo Books, an imprint of William Morrow & Co., 1350 Avenue of the Americas, New York, NY 10019 by arrangement with Random House UK, Ltd.

Printed in Hong Kong

10 9 8 7 6 5 4 3

INTRODUCTION

Make a world of animals out of plain paper!

Using simple paper-folding know-how, *Origami Safari* takes you on an amazing journey from the Northern Polar regions to the Australian outback – and to dozens of places in between! Learn how to make elephants, tigers, monkeys, and other wonderful, wild creatures – just by folding squares of paper. There are plenty of sheets enclosed right here in this book to get you started.

After you have used the paper included here, you can choose almost any other kind of paper to make more animals. You can buy special origami paper – colored on one side, white on the other – from department stores, toy shops, stationery shops, Asian gift shops, and art-supply stores. You can also use wrapping paper or pages from magazines. You can even cut origami squares from the Sunday comics!

With *Origami Safari*, you can also create environments for your animal figures. Start by copying the arrangements that appear in the photographs, but don't be afraid to develop these suggestions in your own way. All you need to create a lifelike scene is a few pieces of cardstock, scissors, glue, and your own imagination.

Before you tackle the actual figures, take a few minutes to master these three special paper-folding techniques: the kite base, used in steps one and two of the PENGUIN model on page 4; and the body units A and B from the MONKEY model on page 11. Squares of paper cut out of newspapers are good to practice with.

Here are some helpful hints about origami:

• Be sure to obtain the right color and kind of paper to match the origami you plan to fold. If you want your figures to look lifelike, choose black and white paper for making the penguin, for example.

• Before you start, make sure your paper is square. It doesn't matter how big the square is, but each side must measure the same length.

• Work on a flat surface, such as a table, drawing table, or book.

• Take the time to make your folds and cuts neat and accurate.

• Press your folds into place by running your thumbnail along each of them.

• Look carefully at the illustrations. The shading represents the colored side of the paper.

• If a fold or a whole model does not work out, don't give up. Put the project aside and come back to it in a few hours or on another day. You may wish to ask someone older than you to help out.

If you want to learn more about origami, contact the Friends of the Origami Center of America, 15 West 77th Street, New York, NY 10024-5192.

Have fun – and happy folding!

CONTENTS

Introduction	page 3
Penguin	page 4
Cobra	page 5
Savanna grass/	
Bamboo leaves	page 7
Seal	page 7
Ostrich	page 9
Monkey	page 11
Zebra	page 13
Tiger	page 15
Lion Family	page 17
Hippopotamus	page 20
Elephant	page 21
Polar Bear	page 22
White Rhinoceros	page 24
Giraffe	page 25
Gazelle	page 26
Red Kangaroo	page 28
Koala	page 30
Giant Panda	page 31

Paper sizes

The most common sizes for origami paper are 12cm (5in) and 15cm (6in) squares, but smaller and larger sizes are also available. A penguin made from a 15cm (6in) square will produce a model 11cm ($4\frac{1}{2}$in) in height. Of course, you can cut your own squares to fit your personal requirements.

PENGUIN

Habitat

Shores of Antarctica and on islands off Australia, New Zealand, South Africa, and southern South America.

Origami folds look most effective when displayed together. So why not try making a display of penguins?

You will need:

Square of paper, black on one side and white on the other

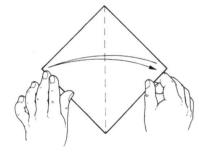

1 Turn the square around to look like a diamond, with the white side on top. Fold and unfold it in half from side to side.

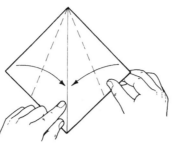

2 From the top point, fold the sloping sides in to meet the middle fold-line, making a shape that in origami is called the kite base.

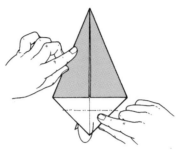

3 Fold the bottom point behind.

4 Fold the middle flaps of paper behind as shown.

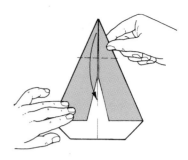

5 Fold the top point down, so making the penguin's head.

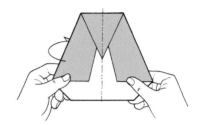

6 Fold the left-hand side behind to the right-hand side.

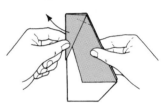

7 Holding the penguin as shown pull its head upwards so it becomes free and sticks out from the folded side.

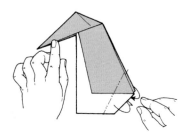

8 Press the top of the penguin's head flat. Fold the bottom right-hand point up inside the model. Repeat behind.

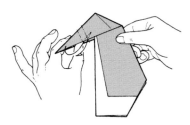

9 Now double inside reverse fold the penguin's head. This is what you do:

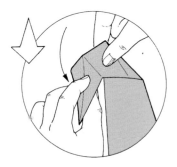

10 Push the head down inside itself as shown.

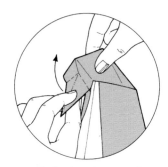

11 Pull the head up as shown. Press the paper flat, so

12 making the penguin's beak.

13 Here is the completed penguin.

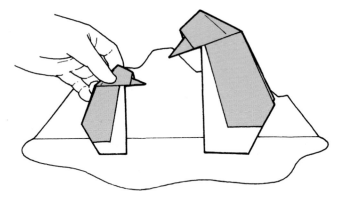

14 As with all of the animals to be found in ORIGAMI SAFARI, try folding a baby penguin from a small square of paper.

COBRA

Habitat
Africa, southern Asia, the Malay Archipelago, and the Philippines.

The folding of this particular model is based around the reverse fold. Even though it may appear difficult at first, the cobra can be folded quite easily.

You will need:
Square of paper, colored on one side and white on the other

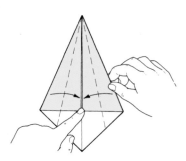

1 Repeat steps 1 and 2 of the PENGUIN on page 4. From the top point, fold the kite base's sloping sides in to meet the middle fold-line.

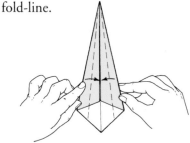

2 Again, from the top point, fold the sloping sides in to meet the middle fold-line.

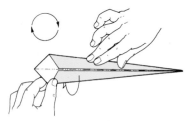

3 Turn the paper around into the position shown. Fold the bottom up behind to meet the top.

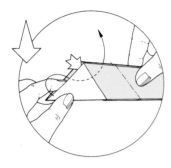

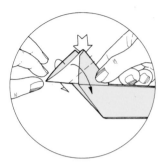

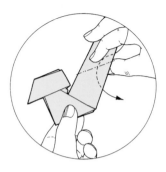

4 Now inside reverse fold the left-hand point. This is what you do:

8 Now outside reverse fold the head. This is what you do: Separate the head's layers of paper,

11 Inside reverse fold the right-hand point down as shown.

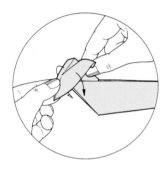

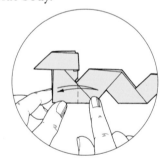

5 Push the left-hand point up inside the model as shown.

9 taking one to the front and one to the back as shown. Press the paper flat, to make the cobra's hood.

12 Repeat steps 10 and 11 a few more times, so making the cobra's body.

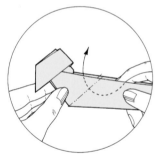

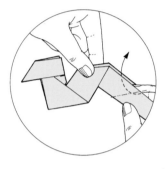

6 Press the paper flat, making the cobra's head.

10 Inside reverse fold the right-hand point up as shown.

13 Fold the head and hood over at an angle. Press them flat and unfold them.

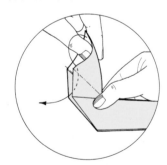

7 Inside reverse fold the cobra's head as shown.

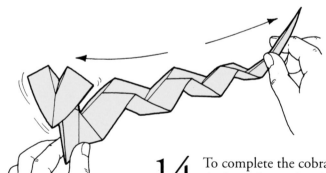

14 To complete the cobra, face the head forward and open out its hood and body slightly.

SAVANNA GRASS/ BAMBOO LEAVES

Habitat

Savanna grass — found in open flat land in warm and sometimes wet parts of the world. Bamboo — a tall plant of the grass family found especially in tropical areas.

Try folding some different sized savanna grasses and bamboo leaves to add something special to your animal scenes.

You will need:

3 squares of paper all the same size, green on one side and white on the other

Glue

Narrow rectangle of green cardstock

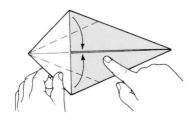

1 GRASS: Repeat steps 1 and 2 of the PENGUIN on page 4 with one square. Turn the kite base around into the position shown. From the left-hand point, fold the short sloping sides in to meet the middle fold-line to make a shape that in origami is called the diamond base.

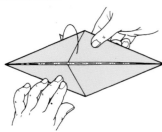

2 Fold the top behind to the bottom.

3 Inside reverse fold the right-hand point as shown.

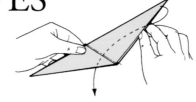

4 This should be the result.

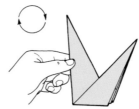

5 To complete the savanna grass, turn it around into the position shown.

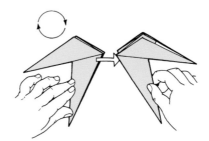

6 BAMBOO LEAVES: Repeat steps 1 to 4 with the remaining two squares. Tuck the savanna grasses inside each other as shown. Glue them together.

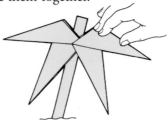

7 To complete the bamboo leaves, glue them on to the narrow rectangle of craft card as shown.

SEAL

Habitat

On or near coasts of all oceans of the world.

You can have a lot of fun folding this model, as well as learning how to fold a very important origami base.

You will need:

2 squares of paper the same size, black, brown, or gray on one side and white on the other
Scissors

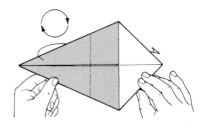

1 FEMALE: Repeat steps 1 and 2 of the PENGUIN on page 4 with one square of paper. Turn the kite base around into the position shown. Fold the left-hand point behind to the right-hand point.

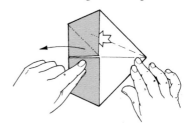

2 Pull the top flap of paper over

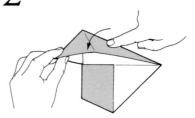

3 to the left, so its sloping edge meets the middle-fold line. Press the paper flat, to

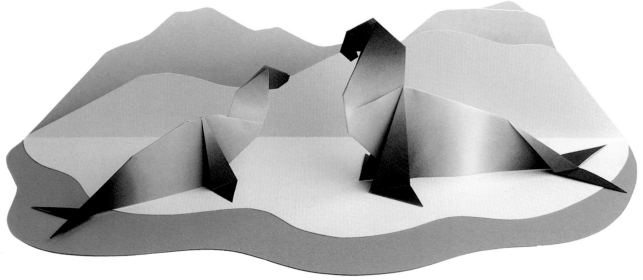

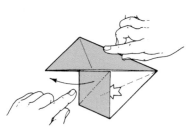

4 make a triangular pointed flap. Repeat steps 2 to 4 with the bottom flap of paper to make a shape that is called the fish base.

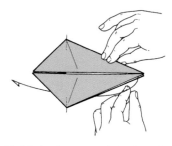

5 Fold the bottom right-hand point to the left as shown.

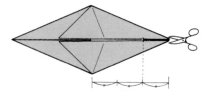

6 From the right-hand point, cut along the middle fold-line as far as shown, to make the seal's back flippers.

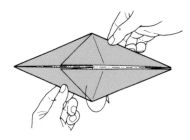

7 Fold the bottom behind up to the top.

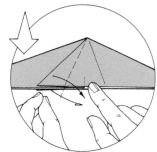

8 Fold the triangular flap over as shown to make a front flipper. Repeat behind.

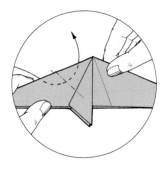

9 Inside reverse fold the left-hand point as shown.

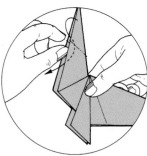

10 Again, reverse fold the left-hand point as shown to make the seal's head.

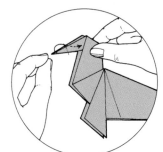

11 Blunt the head with an inside reverse fold.

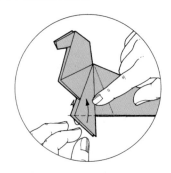

12 Fold the front flipper up. Repeat behind.

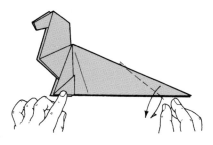

13 Fold the back flipper down. Repeat behind.

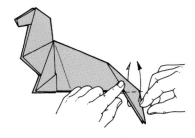

14 Fold the back flipper up. Repeat behind.

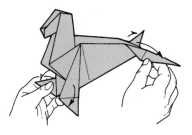

15 To complete the female seal, fold down its front flippers slightly and spread the back ones apart.

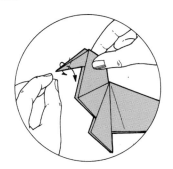

16 MALE: Repeat steps 1 to 10 with the remaining square. Outside reverse fold the head's tip to make a snout. To complete, repeat steps 12 to 15.

OSTRICH

Habitat
The Sahara Desert and the dry table lands of southeastern Africa.

It is possible to make a sitting ostrich if you don't make the ostrich's legs.

You will need:
3 squares of paper all the same size, one square black on both sides for the ostrich's body and two squares white on both sides for its head and legs

Glue

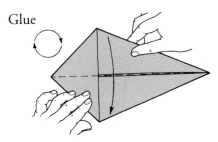

1 BODY: Repeat steps 1 and 2 of the PENGUIN on page 4 with the black square. Turn the kite base around into the position shown. Fold the top down to the bottom.

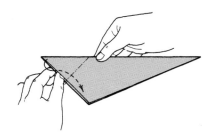

2 Inside reverse fold the left-hand point as shown.

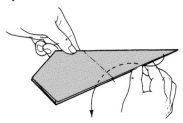

3 Inside reverse fold the right-hand point downwards.

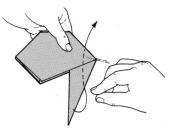

4 Inside reverse fold the right-hand point upwards.

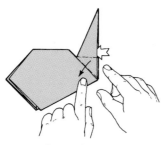

5 Insert a finger between the right-hand point's layers of paper as shown. Open them out and

6 with your free hand, press the paper down into

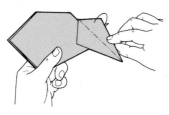

7 a diamond shape. Fold the diamond's upper sloping edges behind as shown,

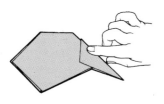

8 completing the body.

9 HEAD: Repeat steps 1 and 2 of the COBRA on page 5 with one white square. Turn the paper around into the position shown. Fold it in half from right to left.

10 Inside reverse fold the top point, to make the ostrich's head.

11 Double reverse fold the head as shown, so

12 making the beak. To complete the head, press it flat.

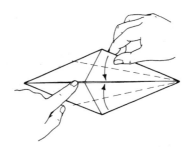

13 LEGS: Repeat step 1 of the SAVANNA GRASS on page 7 with the remaining white square. From the right-hand point, fold the sloping sides in to meet the middle fold-line.

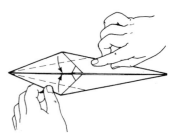

14 From the left-hand point, fold the sloping sides in to meet the middle fold-line.

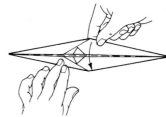

15 Fold the top down to the bottom.

16 Fold in half from right to left.

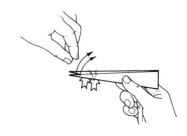

17 Double reverse fold both left-hand points as shown, so making the ostrich's feet. To complete the legs, press them flat.

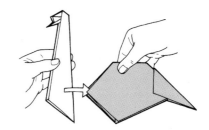

18 OSTRICH ASSEMBLY: Insert the ostrich's head into the body as shown.

19 Treating the inside left-hand points as if they were one, fold them

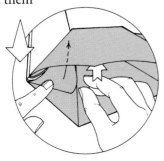

20 up inside the body, locking the head and body together.

21 Insert the ostrich's legs into the body as shown. Glue them together.

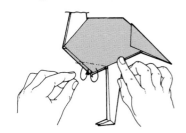

22 Fold the lower left-hand point up inside the body. Repeat behind.

23 Here is the completed ostrich.

MONKEY

Habitat
Forests in Africa, Asia, Mexico through Central and South America.

Nearly all of the animals to be found in ORIGAMI SAFARI are based around the following body units.

You will need:
4 squares of paper all the same size, brown on one side and white on the other

Scissors

Glue

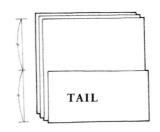

1 TAIL: From one square, cut out a rectangle for the tail to the size shown.

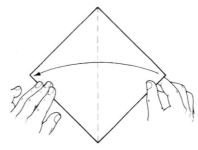

2 BODY UNIT A: Turn one square around to look like a diamond, with the white side on top. Fold it in half from right to left, making a triangle.

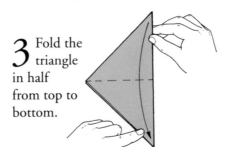

3 Fold the triangle in half from top to bottom.

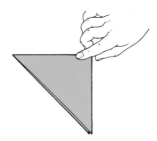

4 To complete body unit A, press it flat.

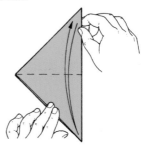

5 BODY UNIT B: Repeat step 2 with another square. Fold and unfold the triangle in half from top to bottom.

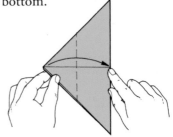

6 Fold the left-hand points over to meet the middle of the right-hand side.

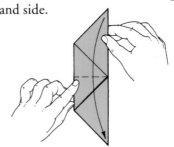

7 Fold in half from top to bottom.

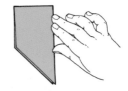

8 To complete body unit B, press it flat.

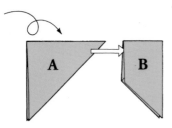

9 Turn body unit A over from side to side. Insert it into body unit B as shown. Glue them together.

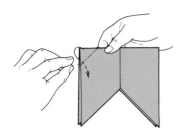

10 To complete the body, inside reverse fold a little of its top left-hand corner.

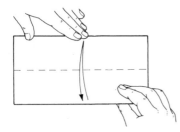

11 TAIL: Place the rectangle sideways, with the white side on top. Fold and unfold it in half from bottom to top.

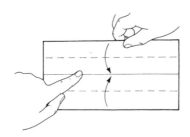

12 Fold the top and bottom edges in to meet the middle fold-line, so making a shape that is called the cupboard fold in origami.

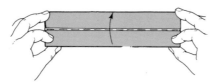

13 Fold in half from bottom to top.

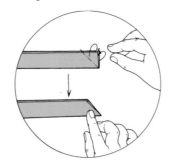

14 Fold the top right-hand corner down inside the cupboard fold. Repeat behind.

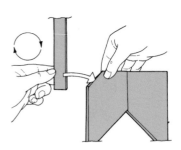

15 Turn the tail around and insert it into the body as shown. Glue them together. Outside reverse fold the tail, so

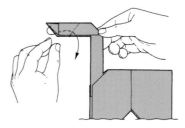

16 that it points towards the left. To complete the tail, inside reverse fold it downwards.

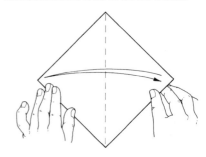

17 HEAD: Turn the remaining square around to look like a diamond, with the white side on top. Fold and unfold it in half from side to side.

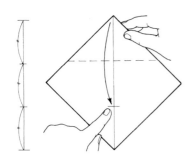

18 Fold the top point down as far as shown.

19 Fold over both the right and left-hand short, sloping sides so that they lie along the top edge.

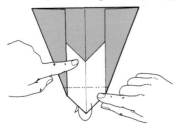

20 Fold the bottom point behind as far as shown.

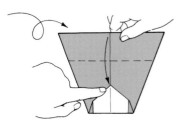

21 Turn the paper over from side to side. Fold the top edge down to meet the bottom point.

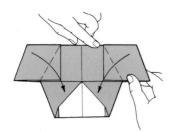

22 Fold the right and left-hand short sloping edges over as shown.

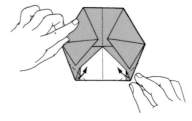

23 Fold over a little of each bottom point.

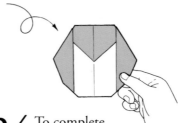

24 To complete the head, turn it over from side to side.

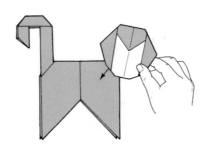

25 To complete the monkey, glue the head on to the body at the desired angle.

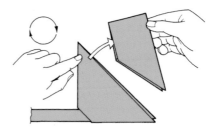

26 To make a sitting monkey, repeat steps 1 to 24, but in step 9 turn body unit A around and insert it into body unit B at an angle as shown. And, in steps 15 and 16, reverse fold the tail to fit your requirements.

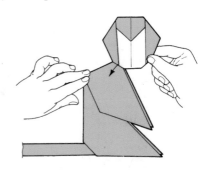

27 To complete, repeat step 25.

ZEBRA

Habitat
Savanna and open forests of eastern Africa.

Do try to fold this origami model accurately. Otherwise, your finished zebra will not look neat and tidy.

You will need:
4 squares of paper all the same size, white on both sides

Scissors

Glue

Black felt-tip pen

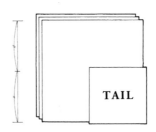

1 TAIL: From one square of paper, cut out a square for the tail to the size shown.

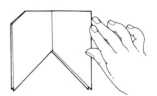

2 BODY: Repeat steps 2 to 10 of the MONKEY on page 11 with two squares.

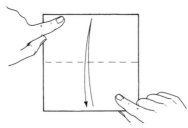

3 TAIL: Fold and unfold the tail's square in half from bottom to top.

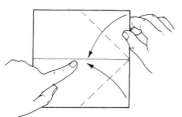

4 Fold the top and bottom right-hand corners in to meet the middle fold-line.

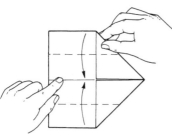

5 Fold the top and bottom edges in to meet the middle fold-line.

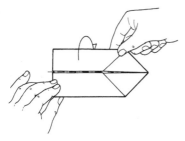

6 Fold the top half behind to the bottom.

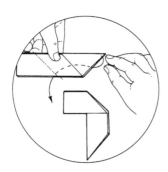

7 Inside reverse fold the right-hand point downwards as shown.

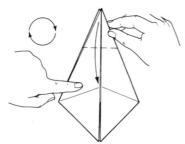

8 To complete the tail, turn it over from side to side. Insert the tail into the body as shown. Glue them together.

9 HEAD: Repeat steps 1 to 4 of the SEAL on page 7 with the remaining square. Turn the fish base around into the position shown. Fold its top point down

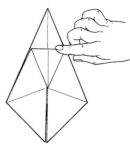

10 as far as shown, to make the zebra's ears.

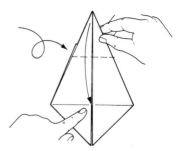

11 Turn the paper over from side to side. Fold the top point down as far as shown.

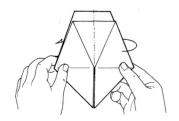

12 Fold the right-hand side behind to the left-hand side.

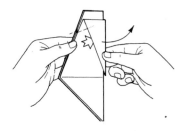

13 Holding the paper as shown, pull the point upwards so it becomes free and sticks out from the folded side.

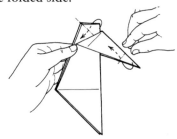

14 Blunt the point and shape the ears with inside reverse folds as shown.

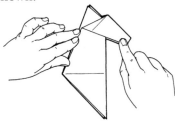

15 Here is the completed head.

16 Glue the head onto the body as shown. To complete the zebra, draw on its stripes with black felt-tip pen.

TIGER

Habitat
Variable, including most forests in Asia from India north and east to Siberia, and then south to Java.

When making this model try hard to find the right paper color.

You will need:
4 squares of paper all the same size, orange on one side and white on the other

Scissors

Glue

Black felt-tip pen

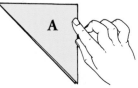

1 From two pieces of origami paper, cut a square for the head and a rectangle for the tail. Look at the diagram above to judge the sizes.

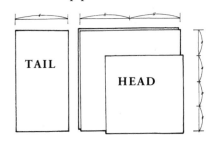

2 BODY UNIT A: Repeat steps 2 to 4 of the MONKEY on page 11 with one square.

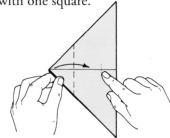

3 BODY UNIT B: Repeat step 5 of the MONKEY on page 11 with the remaining square. Fold the left-hand points over as far as shown.

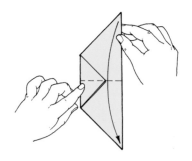

4 To complete body unit B, fold it in half from top to bottom.

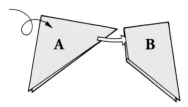

5 Turn body unit A over from side to side. Insert it into body unit B at a sloping angle as shown. Glue them together.

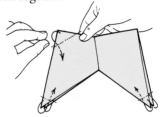

6 To complete the tiger's body, inside reverse fold a little of its top left-hand corner and bottom points as shown.

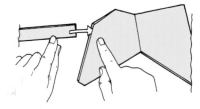

7 TAIL: Repeat steps 11 to 14 of the MONKEY on page 12 with the tail's rectangle. Insert the tail into the body as shown. Glue them together.

8 To complete the tail, inside reverse fold it upwards.

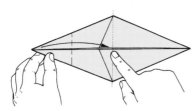

9 HEAD: Repeat step 1 of the SAVANNA GRASS on page 7, using the square of paper for the head. Fold the left-hand point in to the diamond base's middle.

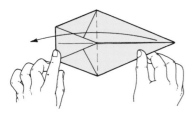

10 Fold the right-hand point over to the left on a line between the top and bottom points.

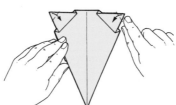

11 Turn the paper around into the position shown. Fold the top points down and then back up, so making small pleats.

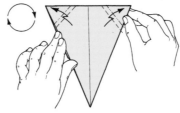

12 Fold over a little of each top point.

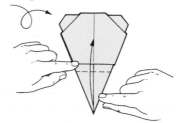

13 Turn the paper over from side to side. Fold the bottom point up as far as shown.

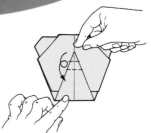

14 Fold the point over, and over again.

15 To complete the head, fold behind a little of each bottom point.

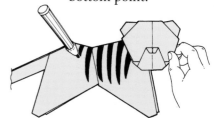

16 Glue the head on to the body at the desired angle. To complete the tiger, draw on its stripes with the black felt-tip pen.

LION FAMILY

Habitat
The African savanna and scrub; in India and Asia, it has adapted to forest life.

As each member of the lion family is made up of similar units, be very careful not to get the folding steps mixed up.

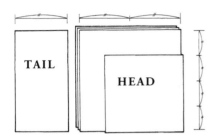

1 MALE: Fold and unfold one square in half from side to side. Cut along the middle fold-line, so making two rectangles. Put one rectangle to one side as it will be required for the female's tail. From another square, cut out a square for the head to the size shown.

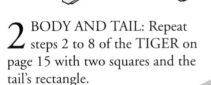

2 BODY AND TAIL: Repeat steps 2 to 8 of the TIGER on page 15 with two squares and the tail's rectangle.

You will need:
MALE - 5 squares of paper all the same size, brownish yellow on one side and white on the other
FEMALE - 3 squares of paper the same size and color as the male's squares
CUB - 4 squares of paper that are half the size of and the same color as the male's squares
Scissors
Glue

3 HEAD: Repeat steps 9 to 15 of the TIGER on page 16 with the head square.

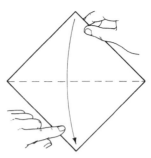

4 MANE: Turn the remaining square around to look like a diamond, with the white side on top. Fold it in half from top to bottom to make an upside-down triangle.

5 Fold and unfold the triangle in half from side to side.

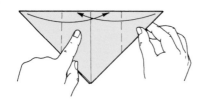

6 Fold the top points over, so that they overlap.

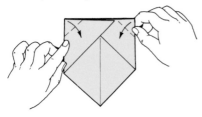

7 Fold over a little of each top point.

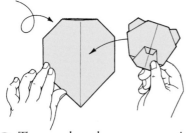

8 To complete the mane, turn it over from side to side. Glue the male's head on to the mane as shown.

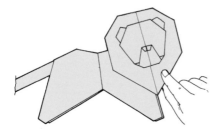

9 To complete the male, glue the mane onto the body at the desired angle.

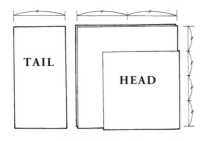

10 FEMALE: Cut out a square for the head to the size shown.

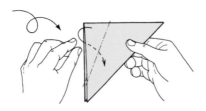

11 BODY UNIT A: Repeat steps 2 to 4 of the MONKEY on page 11 with one square. Turn body unit A over from side to side. To complete unit A, inside reverse fold its top left-hand point as shown.

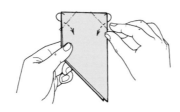

12 Body unit B: Repeat steps 5 to 8 of the MONKEY on page 11 with the remaining square. To complete body unit B, inside reverse fold a little of each top point as shown.

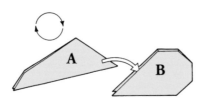

13 Turn body unit A around. Insert it into body unit B as shown. Glue them together.

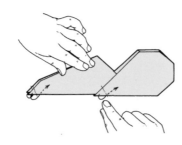

14 To complete the body, inside reverse fold the points as shown. Repeat behind.

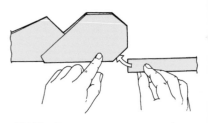

15 TAIL: Repeat steps 11 to 14 of the MONKEY on page 12 with the tail's rectangle (see step 1). Insert the tail into the body as shown. Glue them together.

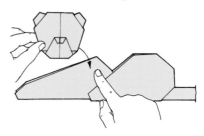

16 HEAD: Repeat steps 9 to 15 of the TIGER on page 16 with the square for the head. To complete the female, glue the head onto the body at the desired angle.

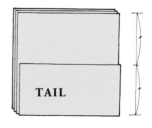

17 CUB: From one square, cut out the rectangle for the tail to the size shown.

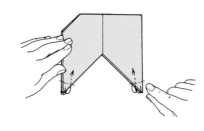

18 BODY: Repeat steps 2 to 10 of the MONKEY on page 11 with two squares. To complete the body, inside reverse fold the bottom points as shown. Repeat behind.

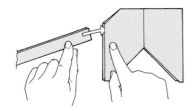

19 TAIL: Repeat steps 11 to 14 of the MONKEY page 12, using the rectangle (see step 17). Insert the tail into the body as shown. Glue them together.

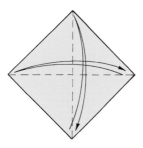

20 HEAD: Fold the remaining square's opposite corners and points together in turn to mark the diagonal fold-lines, with the colored side on top, then open up again.

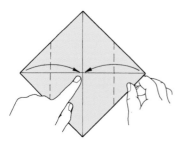

21 Fold the right- and left-hand corners in to meet the middle.

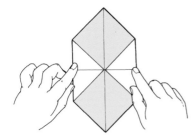

22 This should be the result.

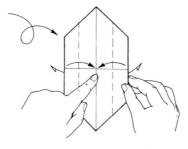

23 Turn the paper over from side to side. Fold the sides in to meet the middle, while at the same time letting the corners from underneath flick up.

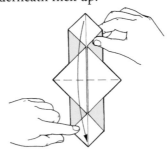

24 Fold the paper in half from top to bottom.

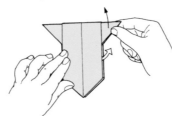

25 Pull the right-hand point up

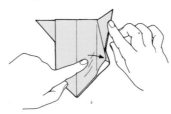

26 as far as shown to make an ear. Press the paper flat.

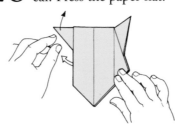

27 Repeat steps 25 and 26 with the left-hand point.

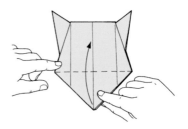

28 Fold the bottom points up.

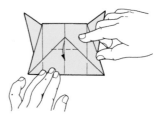

29 Fold the bottom points back down to make a small upside down triangle.

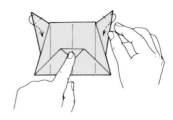

30 Inside reverse fold the ears as shown.

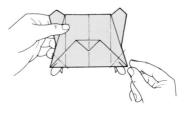

31 To complete the head, fold the lower right- and left-hand side points behind.

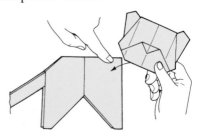

32 To complete the cub, glue the head onto the body at the desired angle.

HIPPOPOTAMUS

Habitat
In rivers and lakes, surrounded by grassland, sub-Saharan Africa.

This model is very easy to fold. Do not be discouraged by the tricky folds in steps 4 to 7; they all fall into place very easily.

You will need:
3 squares of paper all the same size, gray on one side and white on the other

Scissors

Glue

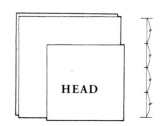

1 HEAD: From one square cut out a square for the head to the size shown.

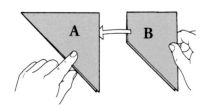

2 BODY UNITS A AND B: Repeat steps 2 to 4 of the TIGER on page 15 with the remaining two squares. Insert body unit B into body unit A as shown. Glue them together.

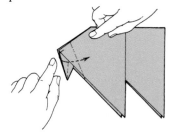

3 Inside reverse fold the left-hand point.

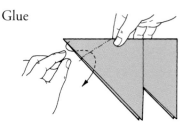

4 Narrow down the reversed point. This is what you do:

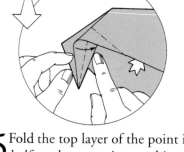

5 Fold the top layer of the point in half, at the same time pushing the triangular area inwards as shown by the line of dots and dashes.

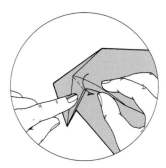

6 This shows step 5 taking place.

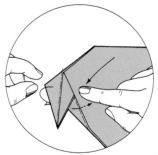

7 Repeat steps 4 to 6 behind to make the hippopotamus's tail.

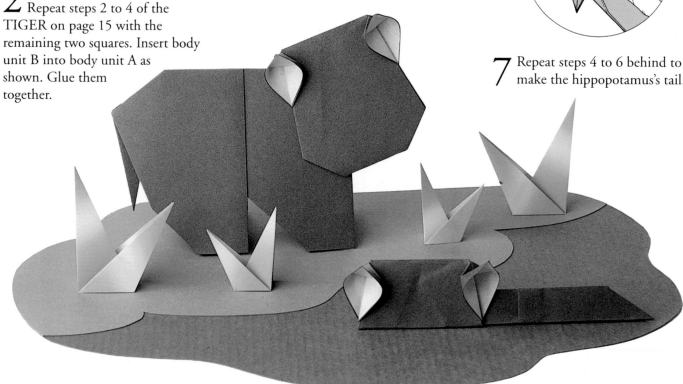

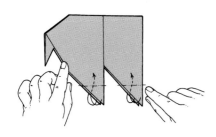

8 To complete the body, inside reverse fold the bottom points as shown.

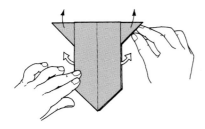

9 HEAD: Repeat steps 20 to 24 of the LION CUB on page 19 with the head's square. Pull each top point up

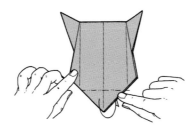

10 as far away as shown to make the ears. Fold the bottom points behind.

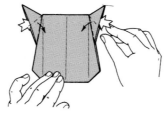

11 Open out each ear and press it down neatly into a diamond shape.

12 Open out each ear, so that it

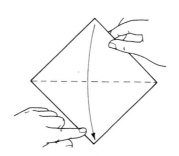

13 becomes three-dimensional as shown.

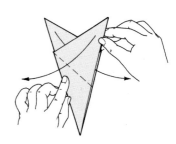

14 To complete the hippopotamus, glue the head on to the body at the desired angle.

ELEPHANT

Habitat
Semidesert; forest to plains of Africa, India, the Indochinese peninsula, Sumatra, and Sri Lanka.

With just a few folds you can make a marvelous elephant.

You will need:
3 squares of paper all the same size, gray on one side and white on the other

Glue

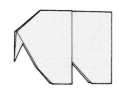

1 BODY: Repeat steps 2 to 8 of the HIPPOPOTAMUS on page 20, using 2 squares.

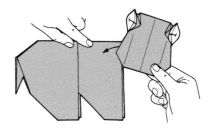

2 HEAD: Turn the remaining square around to look like a diamond, with the white side on top. Fold it in half from top to bottom to make an upside down triangle.

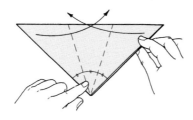

3 Fold the right-hand side over to a point one-third of the way across the triangle. Repeat with the left-hand side so that it lies on top.

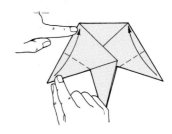

4 Fold the top points over to either side to make the ears.

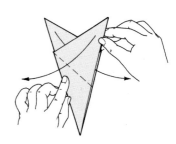

5 Fold the ears in half as shown.

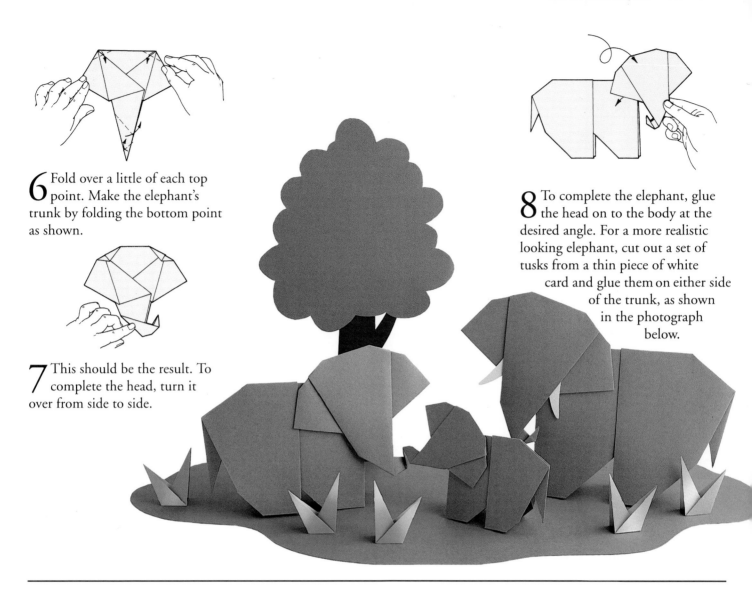

6 Fold over a little of each top point. Make the elephant's trunk by folding the bottom point as shown.

7 This should be the result. To complete the head, turn it over from side to side.

8 To complete the elephant, glue the head on to the body at the desired angle. For a more realistic looking elephant, cut out a set of tusks from a thin piece of white card and glue them on either side of the trunk, as shown in the photograph below.

POLAR BEAR

Habitat

The snow and ice fields of the Northern Polar regions.

By using different shades of paper it is possible to make many different species of bears.

You will need:

3 squares of paper all the same size, white on both sides

Glue

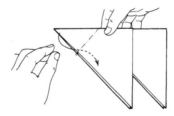

1 BODY: Repeat step 2 of the HIPPOPOTAMUS on page 20 with two squares. Inside reverse fold the left-hand point.

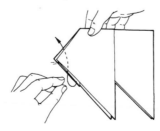

2 Reverse fold the point back out, making the polar bear's tail.

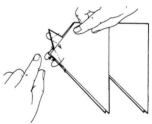

3 Blunt the tail with an inside reverse fold. Fold the left-hand side point inside the body. Repeat behind.

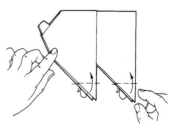

4 Fold the bottom points up. Repeat behind.

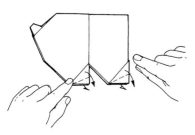

5 Fold the bottom points down as shown to make the paws. Repeat behind.

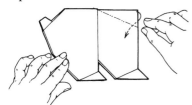

6 To complete the body, inside reverse fold the top right-hand point as shown.

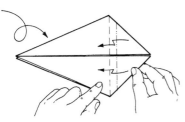

7 HEAD: Repeat steps 1 to 4 of the SEAL on page 7 with the remaining square. Turn the fish base over from side to side. Fold the top and bottom triangular points to the left and back to the right, making small pleats.

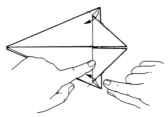

8 Fold the top and bottom points over the pleats.

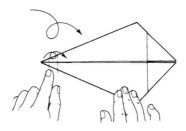

9 Turn over from top to bottom. Treating the left-hand side points as if they were one, fold them over and over again to make the bear's nose.

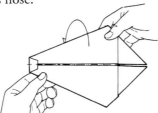

10 Fold the top behind the bottom.

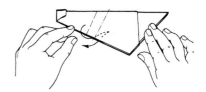

11 Double reverse fold the nose as shown (see steps 9 to 11 of the PENGUIN on page 5).

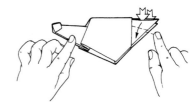

12 To complete the head, open out the right-hand points slightly, so making the ears.

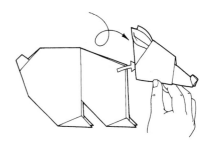

13 Turn the head over. To complete the polar bear, glue the head onto the body at the desired angle.

WHITE RHINOCEROS

Habitat

African grasslands and savanna; also near swamps and rivers in the southern Sudan and South Africa.

The white rhinoceros is actually light gray in color so try to use the correct colored paper.

You will need:

3 squares of paper all the same size, light gray on one side and white on the other

Glue

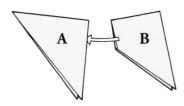

1 BODY UNITS A AND B: Repeat steps 2 to 4 of the TIGER on page 15 with two squares. Insert body unit B into body unit A at a sloping angle as shown. Glue them together.

2 Repeat steps 3 to 7 of the HIPPOPOTAMUS on page 20 to make the tail.

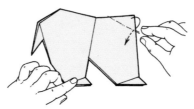

3 Repeat steps 4 and 5 of the POLAR BEAR on page 22 to make the feet. To complete the body, inside reverse fold the top right-hand point as shown.

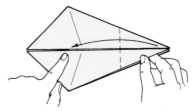

4 HEAD: Repeat steps 1 to 5 of the SEAL on page 7 with the remaining square. Fold the top right-hand point over as far as shown to make the back horn.

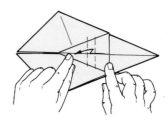

5 Fold the back horn to the right and back to the left to make a small pleat.

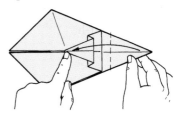

6 Fold the bottom right-hand point over as far as shown to make the front horn.

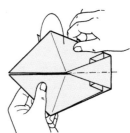

7 Fold the top behind to the bottom.

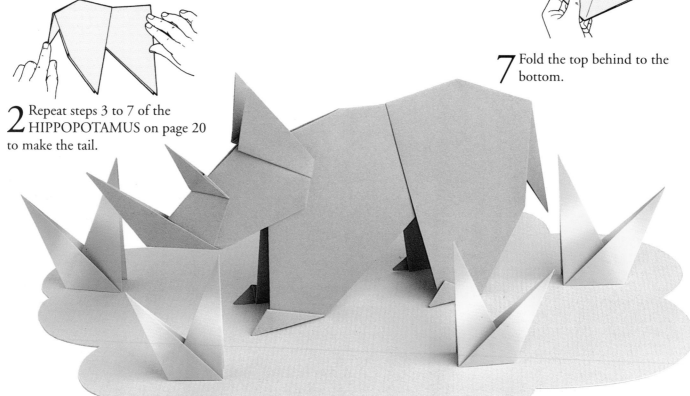

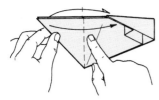

8 Fold the left-hand triangular flap over to the right. Repeat behind.

9 Fold the triangular flap over to meet the left-hand side to make an ear. Repeat behind.

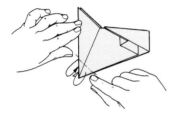

10 Fold the lower left-hand point up inside the head. Repeat behind.

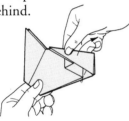

11 Pull the front horn up, pressing it flat into the position shown in step 12.

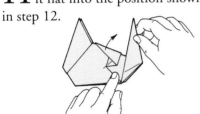

12 To complete the head, pull the back horn up, pressing it flat into the position shown in step 13.

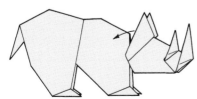

13 To complete the white rhinoceros, glue the head on to the body at the desired angle.

GIRAFFE

Habitat
The savanna and sparse scrub of sub-Saharan Africa.

By making slight variations in the folds, you can easily create a running or feeding giraffe.

You will need:
3 squares of paper all the same size, yellow on one side and white on the other

Glue

Brown felt-tip pen

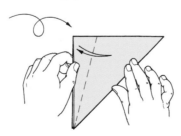

1 BODY: Repeat steps 2 to 4 of the MONKEY on page 11 with one square. Turn the unit over from side to side. Fold and unfold the unit's left-hand side, as shown.

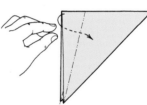

2 Using the fold-lines made in step 1 as a guide, inside reverse fold the unit's left-hand side. Repeat steps 1 and 2 with another square.

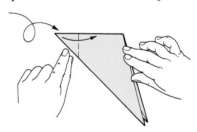

3 Turn one unit over from side to side. Fold the top left-hand point over towards the right.

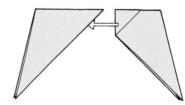

4 Insert one unit inside the other as shown. Glue them together.

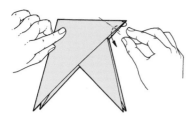

5 To complete the body, inside reverse fold the right-hand point to make the tail.

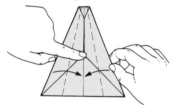

6 HEAD: Repeat steps 1 and 2 of the PENGUIN on page 4 with the remaining square. Fold over a little of the top point. Fold the white triangle up along the base of the colored triangle.

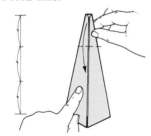

7 From the top edge, fold the sloping sides in to meet the middle fold-line.

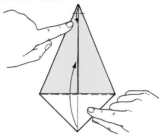

8 Fold the top edge over as far as shown to make the head.

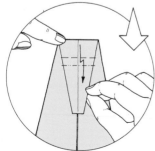

9 Fold the head up and then back down to make a small pleat.

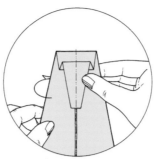

10 Fold the left-hand side behind to the right-hand side.

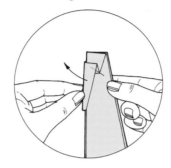

11 Pull up the head as far as the pleat will allow you.

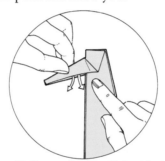

12 Pull out the head's inside layer of paper. Repeat behind.

13 To complete the head, inside reverse fold the top left-hand point to make the ears.

14 Glue the head onto the body at the desired angle.

15 To complete the giraffe, draw on its spots with the brown felt-tip pen.

GAZELLE

Habitat
Desert, to the edge of the Sahel - Saharan Africa.

Remember to fold neatly and look very carefully at each illustration to see what you should do.

You will need:
3 squares of paper all the same size, reddish brown on one side and white on the other

Glue

Scissors

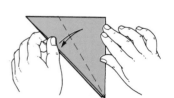

1 BODY: Repeat steps 2 to 4 of the MONKEY on page 11 with one square. Fold and unfold the unit's left-hand sloping side as shown.

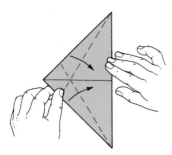

2 Unfold the unit from bottom to top to make a triangle. Using the fold-lines made in step 1 as a guide, fold over the triangle's sloping sides.

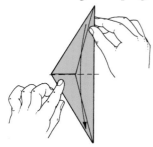

3 Fold the triangle in half from top to bottom to make the gazelle's back legs.

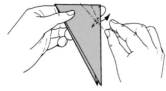

4 Double reverse fold the top right-hand corner of the legs as shown to make the tail.

5 Repeat step 5 of the MONKEY on page 11 with another square. Fold and unfold the triangle in half from left to right.

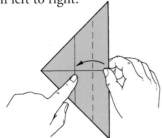

6 Fold the triangle's right-hand side over to meet the fold-line made in step 5.

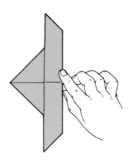

7 This should be the result.

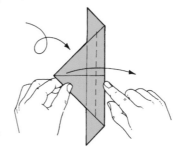

8 Turn the paper over from top to bottom. Fold the left-hand point over, so that the fold-line made in step 5 lies along the right-hand side.

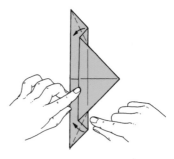

9 Fold the top and bottom right-hand points over as shown.

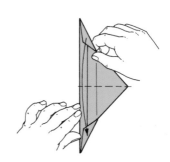

10 Fold in half from top to bottom to make the front legs.

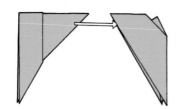

11 Insert the front legs into the back legs as shown. Glue them together.

12 Here is the completed body.

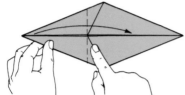

13 HEAD: Repeat step 1 of the SAVANNA GRASS on page 7 with the remaining square. Fold the left-hand point over as shown.

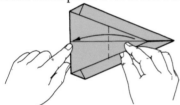

14 Fold the point back out to meet the left-hand side.

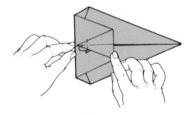

15 Fold behind a little of the point to make the gazelle's head.

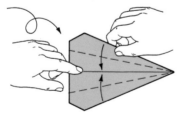

16 Turn the paper over from top to bottom. From the right-hand point, fold the long, sloping sides in to meet the middle fold-line, so as to open out the adjoining left-hand side points.

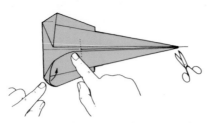

17 Press the points down neatly into triangles. From the right-hand point, cut along the middle fold-line as far as shown to make the gazelle's horns.

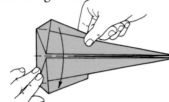

18 Fold in half from top to bottom.

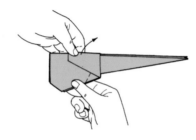

19 Pull up the head and press it flat, into the position shown in step 20.

RED KANGAROO

Habitat
The arid grassland, scrub, and salt plains throughout inland continental Australia.

As with all origami animals, try changing the angle of the folds especially those of the tail, legs, and ears, to see how many new animals you can create.

You will need:
3 squares of paper all the same size, reddish brown on one side and white on the other

Glue

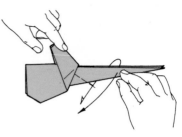

20 Fold the front horn over as shown. Repeat behind.

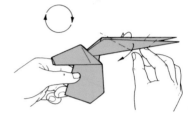

21 Turn the head around into the position shown. To complete the head, shape the horns by folding them down and then back up.

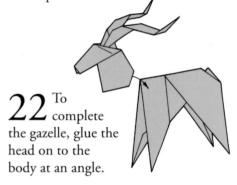

22 To complete the gazelle, glue the head on to the body at an angle.

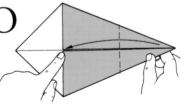

1 BODY: Repeat steps 1 and 2 of the PENGUIN on page 4 with one square. Turn the kite base around into the position shown. Fold the right-hand point over to where the vertical edges and middle fold-line intersect.

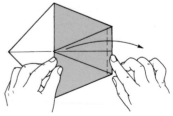

2 Fold the point back out towards the right to make a small pleat.

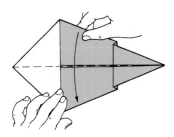

3 Fold in half from top to bottom.

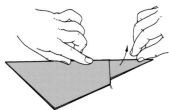

4 Pull up the point as far as the hidden pleat will allow you, to make the kangaroo's tail.

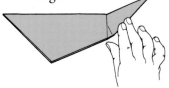

5 To complete the body, press the paper flat.

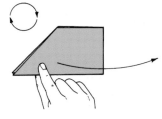

6 BACK LEGS: Repeat steps 5 to 8 of the MONKEY on page 11 with another square. Turn body unit B around into the position shown. Open it out from left to right.

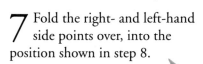

7 Fold the right- and left-hand side points over, into the position shown in step 8.

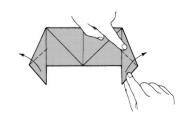

8 Fold the points back up, into the position shown in step 9.

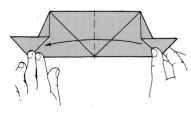

9 To complete the back legs, fold them in half from right to left.

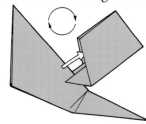

10 Insert the body into the back legs as shown. Glue them together.

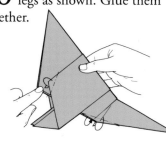

11 To complete the body, shape the tail by folding its bottom points up inside and the legs by folding their top points behind as shown.

12 HEAD AND FRONT PAWS: Repeat steps 9 to 15 of the ZEBRA on page 14 with the remaining square. Fold the triangular pointed flaps towards the left. Press them flat and unfold them.

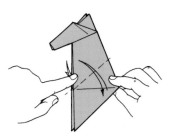

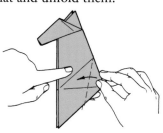

13 Fold the right-hand side point over as shown. Repeat behind.

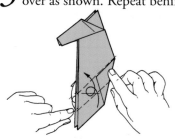

14 To complete the head, fold the triangular pointed flaps over, and then over again to make the front paws.

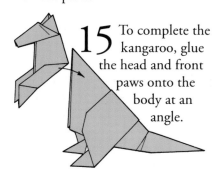

15 To complete the kangaroo, glue the head and front paws onto the body at an angle.

KOALA

Habitat
The eucalypt forest and woodlands of eastern and southwestern coastal Australia.

This koala is a perfect example of an origami technique that uses just a few major folds.

You will need:
2 squares of paper the same size, gray on both sides

Scissors

Glue

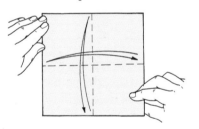

1 HEAD: From one square cut out the head's square to the size shown.

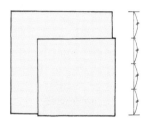

2 BODY: Fold and unfold the remaining square in half from bottom to top and side to side.

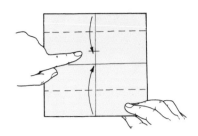

3 Fold the bottom edge in to meet the middle line. Fold the top edge down as far as shown.

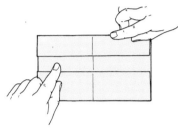

4 This should be the result.

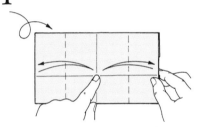

5 Turn the paper over from side to side. Fold the sides in to meet the middle line. Press them flat and unfold them.

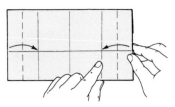

6 Fold the sides in to the fold-lines made in step 5.

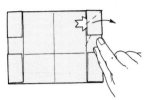

7 Insert your forefinger between the top right-hand layers of paper as shown, and

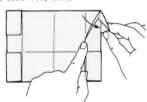

8 open out the top layer.

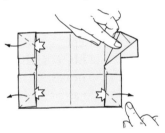

9 Press the paper down neatly into the position shown. Repeat steps 7 to 9 with the bottom right-hand layer and the top and bottom left-hand layers.

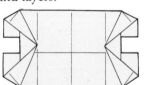

10 This should be the result.

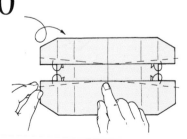

11 Turn the paper over from side to side. Fold each middle point behind as shown.

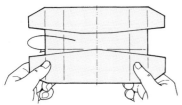

12 Fold the left-hand side behind to the right-hand side.

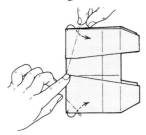

13 To complete the body, inside reverse fold the top and bottom left-hand points as shown.

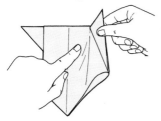

14 HEAD: Repeat steps 20 to 24 of the LION CUB on page 19 with the head's square. Pull each top point up as far as shown to make the ears.

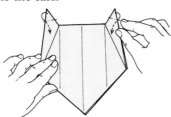

15 Inside reverse fold the tip of each ear.

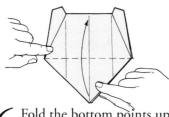

16 Fold the bottom points up as shown to make a triangle.

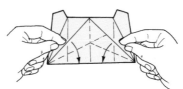

17 Fold the triangle's sloping sides down to meet the bottom edge, while at the same time

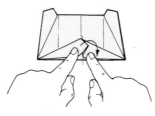

18 flattening the triangle to the right with its sides still folded together to make a triangular flap.

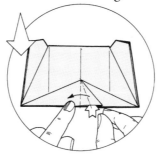

19 Open out the triangular flap and press it down neatly into a diamond.

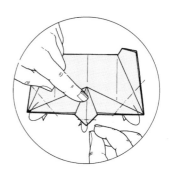

20 Fold behind a little of the diamond's tip. To complete the head, fold the right- and left-hand bottom points behind.

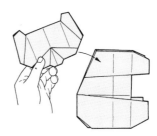

21 To complete the koala, glue the head onto the body at the desired angle.

GIANT PANDA

Habitat
The bamboo forests of south-central China.

This model is very easy to fold and it will bring you plenty of oohs and ahs from your friends!

You will need:
2 squares of paper the same size, black on one side and white on the other

Glue

1 BODY: Repeat steps 2 to 13 of the KOALA on page 30 with one square, but with the white side on top in step 2.

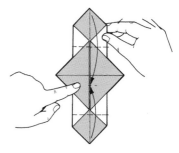

2 HEAD: Repeat steps 20 to 23 of the LION CUB on page 19 with the remaining square, but with the white side on top in step 20. Fold the top and bottom points over as far as shown.

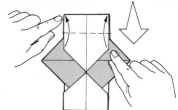

3 Fold the top point back up, so that its side points meet the top edge.

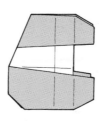

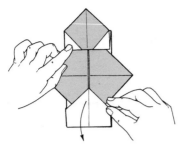

4 Unfold the bottom point.

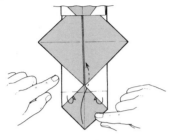

5 Using the fold-lines made in step 2 as a guide, reverse fold the bottom point up inside the model as shown.

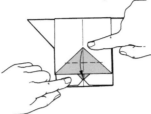

6 Fold the top point down on a line between the two side points.

7 Fold the bottom point up to make a colored triangle.

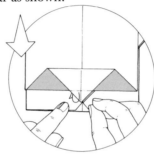

8 Fold the triangle's tip down as far as shown.

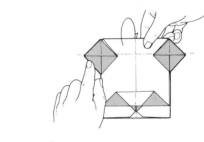

9 Fold the triangle's tip behind up inside the model.

10 Open out each side point and press them down neatly into diamonds.

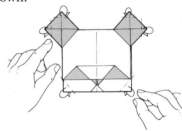

11 Fold one diamond's front flap up, so making an ear. Repeat with the other diamond.

12 Fold the top edge behind on a line between the ears as shown.

13 Shape the ears by folding their top and side points behind. To complete the head, fold the right- and left-hand bottom points behind.

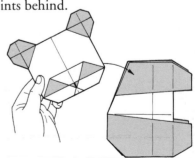

14 To complete the panda, glue the head on to the body at the desired angle.